THE
IRISH
MUSICIANS'
QUOTATION BOOK

THE
IRISH
MUSICIANS'
QUOTATION BOOK

Compiled by Andrew Russell

SOMERVILLE PRESS

Somerville Press Ltd,
Dromore, Bantry, Co. Cork, Ireland

©Andrew Russell 2018
First published 2018

Typeset in Minion Pro

ISBN: 978 0 9955239 13

Printed and bound in Spain
by Graphy Cems, Villatuerta, Navarra

Front cover: Front cover: Bono at U2's concert in Seattle, 2017.
Photograph by Remy.

INTRODUCTION

Ireland is well known for its rich musical tradition stretching back to ancient times, a legacy that continues to be built on today by musicians in all genres. In *The Irish Musicians' Quotation Book* those who have made their names on the world stage reflect on life, love, success and what their art means to them.

I NEVER REALLY WAS A TRADITIONAL SINGER. I CAME FROM THE HEART OF DUBLIN, BUT I HAD A STRONG INTEREST IN TRADITIONAL MUSIC IN THE EARLY DAYS. I THINK THAT LEFT A STRONG MARK ON ME AS A PERFORMER BECAUSE I THINK WHO YOU ARE IN YOUR FORMATIVE YEARS IS THE MAKING OF YOUR STYLE AND WHO YOU BECOME AS AN ARTIST.

Mary Black

OVERCOMING MY DAD TELLING
ME I WOULD NEVER AMOUNT TO
ANYTHING IS WHAT HAS MADE
ME THE MEGALOMANIAC YOU SEE
BEFORE YOU TODAY.

•

MUSIC CAN CHANGE THE WORLD
BECAUSE IT CAN CHANGE PEOPLE.

Bono

As a rock star, I have two instincts. I want to have fun and I want to change the world. I have a chance to do both.

•

I used to love Kurt Cobain, when he was telling people we're a pop band. People would laugh, they thought of it as good old ironic Kurt. But he wasn't being ironic.

Bono

I'M A SINGER, NOT A POLITICIAN
AND I THINK YOU DON'T WANT
TO GET THE TWO CONFUSED. IT'S
NOT OK TO BE ON CNN TALKING
ABOUT PEOPLE STARVING AND
THEN TELL THE INTERVIEWER
THAT YOUR NEW ALBUM IS
COMING OUT IN SIX MONTHS.

Bono

MUSIC FILLS IN FOR WORDS A
LOT OF THE TIME WHEN PEOPLE
DON'T KNOW WHAT TO SAY, AND
I THINK MUSIC CAN BE MORE
ELOQUENT THAN WORDS.

Bono

I'VE ALWAYS HATED THE NOTION
OF FAME, IN A WAY. BUT I KNOW
THAT YOU ALMOST CAN'T HAVE
SUCCESS IN THE MUSIC BUSINESS
UNLESS YOU HAVE A CERTAIN
AMOUNT OF FAME.

Paul Brady

I WAS NEVER FASHIONABLE
ANYWAY, IN TERMS OF IMAGE,
OR WHATEVER. I HAD NO IMAGE.
WHEN YOU SEE SOME OF THE
EARLY VIDEOS OF ME – THE
STUFF ON YOUTUBE – THE STATE
OF ME! I MEAN, REALLY.

Paul Brady

I couldn't get up in the morning if I didn't know God was on my side.

•

When we started Clannad we had no plans to make it big or make a lot of money or find a new sound.

Moya Brennan

'THE LADY IN RED' APPEARS
TO TRANSPORT PEOPLE INTO A
DIFFERENT PLACE, TO INVOLVE
PEOPLE IN A DREAM PERHAPS.

•

LOVE SONGS ARE THE MOST
COMPLEX TO WRITE BECAUSE
EVERYONE KNOWS ABOUT IT.

Chris de Burgh

THEY HAD A BIG INFLUENCE AND
THIS IS A STUNNING ALBUM.

Chris de Burgh
on 'Crime of the Century' by
Supertramp

I'D POSE NAKED FOR A MILLION
POUNDS, BUT I WOULDN'T EAT A
LIVE FISH.

Nicky Byrne
(ex-Westlife)

IF THERE IS ANY JUSTICE IN THE
WORLD, THEN EIGHTIES ROCK
WILL NEVER AGAIN SERVE TO
BLIGHT HUMANITY AS IT DID IN
THAT DARK DECADE.

•

DEF LEPPARD IS A ROCK BAND
THAT CAN SING.

Vivian Campbell
(Def Leppard)

IT'S NOT LIKE NOW WHERE
THINGS ARE DRIVEN BY MONEY
AND GREED . . . IN THE 1960S
THERE WAS A REAL SENSE THAT
SINGING ABOUT THE WORLD
COULD ACTUALLY CHANGE IT.

Liam Clancy

A MAN'S RESPECT FOR LAW
AND ORDER EXISTS IN PRECISE
RELATIONSHIP TO THE SIZE OF
HIS PAY CHEQUE.

Adam Clayton

DON'T GET ME STARTED.
I LOVE IT.

•

FOR US THERE'S U2 MUSIC, AND
THERE'S EVERYTHING ELSE.

Adam Clayton

I COULD NEVER DREAM OF BEING
COOL.

•

I HAVE A HIGH TOLERANCE FOR
DISCOMFORT.

Andrea Corr

EVERYTHING IS NICER IF YOU
FEEL YOU'RE IN LOVE.

•

EVERYONE GETS TOO DRUNK
SOMETIMES; AND EVEN IF
EVERYBODY DIDN'T, I HAVE
GOTTEN TOO DRUNK SOMETIMES.

Andrea Corr

MUSICIANS ARE PROBABLY THE
MOST UNCOMFORTABLE PEOPLE
IN THEMSELVES IN THE WORLD.
HAPPINESS, I THINK, ONLY
EXISTS WHEN YOU'RE A CHILD
AND ONCE YOU GO PAST 11,
UNFORTUNATELY IT'S GONE.

Andrea Corr

I PRAY CONSTANTLY. I HAVE
AN ALTAR.

•

I STILL DON'T THINK WOMEN ARE
TREATED EQUALLY, AND I THINK
IRELAND IS GETTING WORSE.

Mary Coughlan

A SONG IS COMMUNICATING
WITH PEOPLE. ENTERTAINMENT
IS A DIFFERENT AREA.

•

I'VE ALWAYS CONSIDERED MYSELF
A FAILURE: I FEEL I'VE NEVER
DONE ANYTHING RIGHT.

•

I WOULDN'T CALL MYSELF AN
ACTOR OR A SINGER FOR THAT
MATTER, JUST A JOURNEYMAN.

Ronnie Drew

I CAN HOLD A NOTE AND I KNOW
I'M NOT UGLY SO, IN WAYS, THAT'S
ENOUGH

Keith Duffy
(Boyzone)

You see, rock and roll isn't a career or hobby – it's a life force. It's something very essential.

The Edge

Jazz came out of New Orleans, and that was the forerunner of everything. You mix jazz with European rhythms, and that's rock n' roll really. You can make the argument that it all started on the streets of New Orleans with the jazz funerals.

The Edge

U2 ALBUMS NEVER GET
FINISHED. THEY JUST GET
RELEASED.

•

JAMMING IS REALLY THE
MOST AWFUL, EXCRUCIATING
EXPERIENCE FOR ME; I REALLY
DON'T ENJOY IT.

The Edge

I'm not reclusive. I just have a private life.

•

Fame and success are very different things.

Enya

SINGING IN GAELIC IS A VERY,
VERY NATURAL THING TO DO.
I THINK IT LENDS ITSELF VERY
MUCH SO TO BEING SUNG.

Enya

THE PERSONAL APPEARANCES
AND RED CARPET EVENTS ARE
VERY GLITZY, BUT IT'S A BIT
FALSE.

•

WHEN I WAS GROWING UP, I'D BE
IN THE CHOIR. MY MUM WAS THE
ORGANIST IN THE CHURCH, SO I'D
SING IN THE CHURCH.

Enya

I WAS BORN A BOY AND REMAIN
ONE EVER SINCE. FRIENDS AND
RELATIVES OFTEN URGE ME TO
GROW UP AND TAKE AN INTEREST
IN POLITICS, WHISKEY, RACE
MEETINGS, FOREIGN SECURITIES,
POOR RATES, OPTIONS AND
OTHER THINGS THAT MEN TALK
ABOUT, BUT NO – I AM STILL
THE SMALL BOY MESSING ABOUT
WITH A PAINT-BOX

Percy French

My heart is very much in the old traditional music of the 1920s.

Frankie Gavin
(De Dannan)

To me the rhythm is almost everything. It's the hypnotic part of Irish music that takes you to another place.

Frankie Gavin
(De Dannan)

ACTUALLY TODAY I HAD
TO DEFEND THE BUSH
ADMINISTRATION IN FRANCE
AGAIN. THEY REFUSED TO
ACCEPT, BECAUSE OF THEIR
POLITICAL IDEOLOGY, THAT HE
HAS ACTUALLY DONE MORE THAN
ANY AMERICAN PRESIDENT FOR
AFRICA.

Bob Geldof

AND WHEREAS WOMEN HAD
TO FIGHT THEIR WAY INTO THE
WORKFORCE, MEN ARE NOW
FIGHTING TO RECLAIM THEIR
PLACE.

Bob Geldof

IRISH AMERICANS ARE NO MORE
IRISH THEN BLACK AMERICANS
ARE AFRICANS.

Bob Geldof

90% OF DIVORCES ARE INITIATED
BY WOMEN. THAT IS REALLY
ODD. WHY? WHAT'S GOING ON?
WHAT'S THE GREAT DISCONTENT
AT THE HEART OF IT?

Bob Geldof

HARDLY A DAY GOES BY
WITHOUT ME PUTTING A MUDDY
WATERS RECORD ON.

Rory Gallagher

I DON'T REMEMBER A TIME
WHEN I WASN'T SINGING AND
IT WAS JUST ALWAYS PART
OF MY DAY.

Lisa Hannigan

IF YOU WANT EVERYTHING YOU
WRITE TO BE GOOD, YOU WILL
NEVER WRITE ANYTHING.

Lisa Hannigan

I ALWAYS GET EVERYTHING
WRONG ON STAGE. THE
AUDIENCE LOVE IT.

Neil Hannon

My records haven't really
sold in the States and
I don't mind.

Neil Hannon

I SWING FROM STRANGE
HUMILITY TO EGO-CENTRIC
MADNESS.

Neil Hannon

I DON'T SEE HOW YOU GET USED
TO PEOPLE SCREAMING IN YOUR
FACE, AND ANYONE WHO SAYS
DIFFERENT IS LYING.

Niall Horan
(One Direction)

FANS ALWAYS TELL ME I'M
BEAUTIFUL, BUT NO ONE WILL
EVER BE AS BEAUTIFUL AS THEM.

Niall Horan
(One Direction)

I DON'T LIKE FALSE HAPPY
ENDINGS, AND I DON'T THINK
THE REAL WORLD IS SUCH A
FORGIVING PLACE.

Hozier

I LOOK AT ALL GOOD THINGS
WITH A BIT OF A DARK LENS,
I SUPPOSE, ESPECIALLY WITH
SOMETHING LIKE LOVE.

Hozier

REGARDLESS OF THE SEXUAL
ORIENTATION BEHIND A
RELATIONSHIP, IT IS STILL A
RELATIONSHIP AND STILL LOVE

Hozier

THERE A LOT OF RECURRING
THEMES THAT I RESONATED WITH
WHEN I READ *A PORTRAIT OF
THE ARTIST AS A YOUNG MAN*.

Hozier

I AM A FIRM BELIEVER IN GOD. I
WOULDN'T BE RUNNING UP AND
DOWN TO THE CHURCH EVERY
DAY BUT I TALK TO GOD IN MY
OWN WAY.

Dolores Keane

I'VE SIGNED BREASTS AND BUMS.
I'VE SIGNED EVERYTHING!

Ronan Keating

As we all know, the internet is not a true friend of the music industry, but technology is slowly changing that. Soon it will work right for all involved.

Ronan Keating

THE BEE GEES SONGS ARE JUST
TIMELESS. GREAT HOOKS, GREAT
MOMENTS IN THE LYRICS AND
MELODY THAT YOU CAN'T GET
OUT OF YOUR HEAD. ONCE YOU
HEAR ONE OF THEM, YOU'RE
SINGING IT ALL DAY.

Ronan Keating

I THINK I WRITE HONESTLY ABOUT WHAT GOES ON IN A GUY'S MIND, AND GIRLS ARE INTERESTED IN THAT. AS A SEX WE ARE NOT THE BEST COMMUNICATORS WHEN IT COMES TO TALKING ABOUT THE WOMEN IN OUR LIVES. I KNOW I'M NOT – BUT I'M DOING MUCH BETTER WHEN I HAVE A PEN AND PAPER IN MY HAND.

Gary Lightbody
(Snow Patrol)

Anyone who's mechanical
is never a success. If you
haven't any emotion in you,
you have no right being on
the stage, trying to perform
to the public. You couldn't
have any colour in your
work if you were a static
fella. You must be emotional.

Josef Locke

The heartbeat is probably where rhythm originated, but yeah, rhythm is one of my preoccupations, one of the things I love, and Irish music offers loads of opportunity for rhythm.

Donal Lunny

YOU CAN TELL WHEN THE
FINAL SHOW IS COMING UP,
AND PREPARE YOURSELF FOR IT
MENTALLY, BUT WHEN IT FINALLY
COMES UP, IT'S LIKE DREAM. YOU
STAND THERE FEELING THE LOVE
THE AUDIENCE HAVE FOR YOU,
AND YOU THINK 'IS THIS REALLY
GOING TO END?'

Phil Lynott

That's the nice thing about being a live act. I can get the audience. It's like, 'Can I do this tonight?' And you can see when people like you. But on record—and with the pen, it's almost for all time. Really, a lot more thought has to go into it.

Phil Lynott

I'M VERY EASY TO RECOGNISE;
THE DARKIE IN THE MIDDLE
JUMPING AROUND WITH THE
GUITAR, YOU KNOW. DAT BOY
GOT RHYDM!!!

Phil Lynott

I BELIEVE THAT TRUE ART IS
UNIVERSAL IN ITS APPEAL.

John McCormack

I LIVE AGAIN THE DAYS AND
EVENINGS OF MY LONG CAREER. I
DREAM AT NIGHT OF OPERAS AND
CONCERTS IN WHICH I HAVE HAD
MY SHARE OF SUCCESS. NOW LIKE
AN OLD IRISH MINSTREL, I HAVE
HUNG UP MY HARP BECAUSE MY
SONGS ARE ALL SUNG.

John McCormack

LIVE LIFE TODAY AND DEAL WITH
TOMORROW WHEN IT COMES.

Brian McFadden
(ex-Westlife)

I'll know I'm famous when I have five Ferraris, seven houses, Cameron Diaz on my arm, and a little man following me with a huge bag of money.

Brian McFadden
(ex-Westlife)

THE VICTIMS OF SOCIAL
INJUSTICE, SINCE TIME ETERNAL,
HAVE ALWAYS BEEN WITHOUT
THE RESOURCES AND ABILITY
TO FIGHT BACK. THEY ARE
DEFENCELESS AND VOICELESS.

Tommy Makem

WOMEN STAYED SILENT
FAR TOO LONG.

Imelda May

I STILL GET QUESTIONS NOW,
LIKE 'WHO WRITES YOUR SONGS?',
WHICH IS UNBELIEVABLE.

Imelda May

AS A CHILD IT WAS ALWAYS WHAT
I WANTED TO DO.

Samantha Mumba

I WAS CALLED A DIVA—IT
WASN'T REAL.

Samantha Mumba

FOR ME TO GO TO NASHVILLE
WAS LIKE GOING TO ANOTHER
PART OF IRELAND.

Paddy Moloney
(The Chieftains)

IF I HAD TO LIVE AGAIN I WOULD
DO EXACTLY THE SAME THING.
OF COURSE I HAVE REGRETS,
BUT IF YOU ARE 60 YEARS OLD
AND YOU HAVE NO REGRETS, YOU
HAVEN'T LIVED.

Christy Moore

FORTY YEARS AGO, MY LIFE IN MUSIC WAS SUBSTANTIALLY DIFFERENT TO TODAY. I WENT OUT EVERY NIGHT WITH MY GUITAR SEEKING A PLACE TO SING, A FLOOR ON WHICH TO LIE, SOME LOVE, SOME FOOD, A LOT OF WINE THERE WAS NO BUSINESS, NO GIGS, NO QUESTIONS, NO PR, NO RECORDING. LIFE WAS SIMPLER. I WAS POOR AND YOUNG AND HUNGRY. TODAY I AM A LOT MORE FOCUSED ON THE SONG.

Christy Moore

THE MOST IMPORTANT THING
TO REMEMBER ABOUT DRUNKS
IS THAT DRUNKS ARE FAR MORE
INTELLIGENT THAN NON-
DRUNKS – THEY SPEND A LOT OF
TIME TALKING IN PUBS, UNLIKE
WORKAHOLICS WHO CONCENTRATE
ON THEIR CAREERS AND AMBITIONS,
WHO NEVER DEVELOP THEIR
HIGHER SPIRITUAL VALUES, WHO
NEVER EXPLORE THE INSIDES OF
THEIR HEAD LIKE A DRUNK DOES.

Shane McGowan

I'M JUST FOLLOWING THE IRISH
TRADITION OF SONG-WRITING,
THE IRISH WAY OF LIFE, THE
HUMAN WAY OF LIFE. CRAM AS
MUCH PLEASURE INTO LIFE, AND
RAIL AGAINST THE PAIN YOU
HAVE TO SUFFER AS A RESULT.
OR SCREAM AND RANT WITH
THE PAIN AND WAIT FOR IT TO BE
TAKEN AWAY WITH BEAUTIFUL
PLEASURE....

Shane McGowan

WHEN I'M WRITING A SONG,
IT GIVES ME MORE ACTUAL
PLEASURE TO HEAR SOMEONE
ELSE SING IT THAN DO IT MYSELF.

Shane McGowan

I LOVE PLAYING EVERYWHERE. I
LOVE THAT CONNECTION WITH
A SMALL AUDIENCE AND A QUIET
SHOW, YOU'RE WITH A LOUD
BAND AND PEOPLE ARE SINGING
ALONG AND DANCING SO IT IS A
DIFFERENT KIND OF BUZZ. IT'S
ALL GOOD.

Leo Moran
(The Saw Doctors)

HEARING THE BLUES
CHANGED MY LIFE.

Van Morrison

I LEARNT FROM ARMSTRONG ON
THE EARLY RECORDINGS THAT
YOU NEVER SANG A SONG THE
SAME WAY TWICE.

Van Morrison

BEING FAMOUS WAS EXTREMELY
DISAPPOINTING TO ME. WHEN
I BECAME FAMOUS IT WAS A
COMPLETE DRAG AND IT IS STILL
A COMPLETE DRAG.

Van Morrison

MUSIC IS SPIRITUAL. THE
MUSIC BUSINESS IS NOT.

Van Morrison

WHEN YOU'RE IN THE MUSIC
BUSINESS, EVERYTHING IS VERY
PERSONAL, BECAUSE YOU ARE
INVESTED IN EVERYTHING;
THERE'S A DEEP PERSONAL
ATTACHMENT TO YOUR MUSIC.

Larry Mullen

It's a tough life being a pop star. You know, at the end of the day when you've paid all the bills and put the kids through college and that, there's only enough for a small island in the South Pacific

Larry Mullen

I'M ON FIRE WHEN I'M SINGING.
I'M COMPLETELY IN CHARACTER.
I USE MY SENSE MEMORIES, AND
EVERY SYLLABLE IS MEANT. IT'S A
VERY SPECIAL THING.

Sinéad O'Connor

MY CREATIVE PROCESS IS QUITE
SLOW. I HEAR MELODIES IN
MY HEAD WHILE I'M WASHING
THE DISHES AND I ALLOW MY
SUBCONSCIOUS TO DO THE WORK.

Sinéad O'Connor

I COULD STAND IN THE STREET
AND SING AND GET ENOUGH TO
PAY THE BILLS. I DON'T NEED
MILLIONS OF DOLLARS.

Sinéad O'Connor

When I sing, it's the most solitary state: just me, and the microphone, and the Holy Spirit. It's not about notes and scales, it's about emotion.

Sinéad O'Connor

Never judge someone, especially if you don't know them, because you don't know what they are going through. For all you know, your words could be the last thing they hear before deciding they have had enough.

Danny O'Donoghue
(The Script)

You get older and come to the conclusion that it's a great gig making music. Even if you turn into an old gnarly fart, no one cares what you look like if you write good songs. The only gig is to sing well and perform.

Dolores O'Riordan

I LIVE AS I CHOOSE OR I WILL
NOT LIVE AT ALL.

Dolores O'Riordan

I WOULDN'T LIKE TO BE REBORN
AS SOMEONE ELSE, NOT EVEN FOR
A DAY, I'M SO WORN OUT TRYING
TO BE MYSELF…

Mícheál Ó Súilleabháin

I WANT TO GET COMFORTABLE
WITH MY INSECURITIES UNTIL
I AM NO LONGER INSECURE.
I WANT TO BE COMFORTABLE
IN MY SKIN SO THAT I DO NOT
NEED TO DUMP ANY OF MY
DISCOMFORT ONTO SOMEONE
ELSE IN THE FORM OF JUDGMENT.

Damien Rice

INDEX

Mary Black (1955-)   6
Bono (1960-)   7, 8, 9, 10
Paul Brady (1947-)   11, 12
Moya Brennan (1952-)   13
Chris de Burgh (1948-)   14, 15
Nicky Byrne (1978-)   16
Vivian Campbell (1962-)   17
Liam Clancy (1935-2009)   18
Adam Clayton (1960-)   19, 20
Andrea Corr (1974-)   21, 22, 23
Mary Coughlan (1956-)   24
Ronnie Drew (1934-2008)   25
Keith Duffy (1974 -)   26

The Edge (1961-)   27, 28, 29

Enya (1961-)   30, 31, 32

Percy French (1854-1920)   33

Frankie Gavin (1956-)   34, 35

Bob Geldof (1961-)   36, 37, 38, 39

Rory Gallagher (1948-1995)   40

Lisa Hannigan (1981-)   41, 42

Neil Hannon (1970-)   43, 44, 45

Niall Horan (1993-)   46, 47

Hozier (1990-)   48, 49, 50, 51

Dolores Keane (1953-)   52

Ronan Keating (1977-)   53, 54, 55

Gary Lightbody (1976-)   56

Josef Locke (1917-1999)   57

Donal Lunny (1947-)   58

Phil Lynott (1949-1986)   59, 60, 61

John McCormack (1885-1945)   62, 63
Brian McFadden (1980-)   64, 65
Tommy Makem (1932-2007)   66
Imelda May (1974-)   67, 68
Samantha Mumba (1983-)   69, 70
Paddy Moloney (1938-)   71
Christy Moore (1945-)   72, 73
Shane McGowan (1957-)   74, 75, 76
Leo Moran (1964-)   77
Van Morrison (1945-)   78, 79, 80, 81
Larry Mullen (1961-)   82, 83
Sinéad O'Connor (1966-)   84, 85, 86, 87
Danny O'Donoghue (1979-)   88
Dolores O'Riordan (1971-2018)   89, 90
Micheál Ó Súilleabháin (1950-)   91
Damien Rice (1973-)   92